The Dedalus Press

*Three Songs of Home*

**Tony Curtis**

# Three Songs of Home

## Tony Curtis

**DEDALUS**

The Dedalus Press, Dublin
1998

*The Dedalus Press*
24 The Heath, Cypress Downs, Dublin 6W. Ireland

ISBN 1 901233  14 6 (paper) The Dedalus Press
ISBN 1 901233  15 4 (bound) The Dedalus Press

Cover by Michael Boran

Acknowledgments:
Some of these poems have previously appeared in *Poetry Ire-land Review*, *The Irish Studies Review*, *The Atlanta Review*, *The Literary Review (New Jersey)*, *Cafe Review (North Carolina)*, *New Orleans Journal*, *W.P.Journal*, *Force Ten*, *InCognito*, *Class Act*, *Acorn*. Several poems have been read on RTE Radio 1, Dublin Weekend Radio, Anna Livia Radio. Dun Laoghaire Port Authority used parts of "The Voyage" in their ferry terminal. Thanks also to Paula Meehan, Pat Boran and Theo Dorgan.
The author gratefully acknowledges receipt of a Bursary in Literature from the Arts Council of Ireland in 1995.

Dedalus Books are represented and distributed in the U.K. and Europe by *Signature Book Representation distributed by Littlehampton Book services*, 2-4 Little Peter St., Manchester M15 4PS. In the USA and Canada by *Du-four*, PO Box 7, Chester Springs, Pennsylvania 19425.

Printed in Ireland by Colour Books Ltd.

The Dedalus Press receives financial assistance from
An Chomhairle Ealaíon, The Arts Council, Ireland.

*for Mary and Oisin,*
*for all my family and friends*
*(the living and the dead)*

*I will lift up mine eyes unto the hills,*
*From whence cometh my help.*

*Psalm 121*

# CONTENTS

| 9 | *Redeemed* |
|---|---|
| 11 | All The Mountains |
| 16 | Still Life |
| 18 | Cold Mountain |
| 19 | In Darjeeling |
| 20 | The Border |
| 22 | Air |
| 23 | Lobsang's Story |
| 25 | Prayer Guide |
| 26 | Ghosts In The Air |
| 27 | The Vision |
| 29 | Her Pilgrimage |
| 32 | Bird |
| 33 | Hat |
| 34 | The Journey Home |
| 36 | Night Song |
| 38 | Kulanthapitha |
| 39 | Now that I am almost dead . . . |
| 40 | A Habitable Place |
| 44 | The Apothecary |
| 47 | The Crossing |
| 49 | The Damned |
| 51 | Lobsang's Wife |

| | |
|---|---|
| 53 | Blue Bowl |
| 56 | From a Tibetan Journal |
| 58 | Late November |
| 59 | The Old Tea Road |
| 62 | Bread |
| 64 | Home |
| 65 | Lobsang's Last Wish |
| 66 | Ch'a |
| 68 | Stillness |
| 69 | The Voyage |
| 70 | A Quiet House |

# Redeemed

*for Michael Hartnett*

*After years in the quietest of rooms*
*I have taken to the road again.*
*God, in his wisdom,*
*has left everything unblessed :*
*the withering trees; the bracken*
*that covers the bones of winter;*
*the hawthorn, the blackthorn;*
*the stone walls gone to ruin;*
*the mongrel ditch, the culled fields.*
*I place myself amongst them*
*and feel at home.*

## All The Mountains

I

I have lived all my life
staring out this window
at the mountains of Mourne,
and not until this moment
did they even appear remotely
like the Himalayas,
but there they are now
washed in the magnificent light
of those Eastern peaks.

Is it because at this moment
some burly little man
wrapped in a yak skin
is whistling
'The Mountains of Mourne' ?
or muttering to himself
like a small hill farmer :

"If I had two more beasts
I could marry in June,
then my bed would be
a shelter in the winter nights" ?

## II

I've seen monasteries in the Himalayas
held to the sides of mountains
by snow and the grace of prayer,
and trees adorned with ribbons
that look like lanterns from the valley,
and in the valleys walls made
like those you'd find in Connemara.
Yet, though it is bleak in winter,
and it is always winter,
Tibetans are kind people.
As you pass they wave.
Proud of their cleared land
and their hard work,
they stare after you
until you are out of sight,
leaving you wondering
if they are staring still.


## III

I have heard that if you die
in the Himalayas in winter,
the earth being frozen –
too hard to dig –

your body is placed on stones
until the bones are picked clean
by birds of prey.
Then the skeleton is gathered
and divided amongst the relatives :

the skull for the mother,
the hands for the father,
the feet for a holy man.


## IV

A Lama once told me
there are no ghosts in the Himalayas.
All Heaven might be here,
I thought, and he'd never know,
everything being covered
in cloud, mist and snow.
But then, as if reading my eyes,
he said, "there are no ghosts
because no one ever dies.

"A year after we buried my father
a yak came to the monastery.
I thought it a hairy nuisance,
and went to shoo it from the gate,
but I saw my father in its eyes;
I fed him and blessed him
and he went away.

Here everything, from the marks
on these hands to the hairs
on a dog's tail, is reincarnated :
rain returns as rivers,
snow as mountains,
birds as holy Lamas.
Women rarely die :
deep rivered valleys
and high mountains
mirror their lives.
Children come back
as birds that sing in the wind.
This close to Heaven
even rainbows are the souls
of holy men evaporating.'

He took my hands in his
and uttered a quiet prayer :
a shield of glass to cover my cold
soul. Then I watched him move
slowly off down the valley, until
his saffron robes fluttered open
and a bright bird's wing
lifted him into the mist.

## V

That night, staring out the window
of a Sherpa's hut,
I learned the beauty of a mantra,
*Kantega, Nuptse, Tawchee, Lotse,*
*Ama Dablam, Annapurna, Chomolungma,*
*Carrauntoohill, Maumturk, Mourne.*
I blessed the mountains,
while the mountains blessed me.

## Still Life

When I heard of the Tibetan
who made a clock and then
destroyed it because it would be
yet another distraction,
I wondered

Was he troubled by the ticking?
Was he worried he'd never
be quite sure whether to place it
on a shelf or by the bed?
Maybe he felt he'd always
be getting up to glance
at its slowly changing face
or to settle the hands.

So why did he make the clock?
Was it to see if time moved?
And then – suddenly –
at the first tick, it did,
and he began to wonder :
How long do I work?
What's it take to walk from one
end of the valley to the other?
Does day pass quicker than night?

I can see him now, that quiet man,
stepping away from the table,
taking a deep, slow breath,
as he lifts the hammer and swings
so the cogs, and the ticking,
and the time, vanish in a moment.

### Cold Mountain

*– after Bashō*

From here
I cannot see the road,
and Cold Mountain,
always distant,
is covered in cloud.
Since I was a child
I've longed to reach
its peak,
but what separates us
is a sea -
how deep
I cannot tell.
It, too,
is covered in cloud.

## In Darjeeling

When the old Lama looked
curiously at me,
I thought it was to ask
why I hadn't touched
my yak-butter tea,
or what I thought the hands
of God might be holding
at this hour of the day.
Instead he asked,
in his faltering English,
why Americans found
the mountains so extraordinary.
"They're different," I said.
"Like me, they find them
mystical places."
"Oh!" he said, " and I thought
they were all circling fools.
When I pass them on the hills
they always say 'High!'
And 'Yes', I say, 'Very High',
and promise myself
to light a candle
for their circling souls."
"Father," I said, shaking my head,
"they say 'Hi!' and mean 'Hello!'"
He looked thoughtful for a moment.
"I think I've wasted
a thousand prayers
on a hundred kind greetings.
God must be laughing at Lama Doshi."

## The Border

"Why do you wish to enter Tibet?"
the Chinese border guard asked,
studying my papers;
he was a little man
used to making others feel small.

"I'm a sort of anthropologist,
a behavioural scientist,
(I thought it best not to mention poems)
studying the effects of altitude
on the Sherpas and nomadic tribes,
on anyone who looks down on clouds."

"You should have written," he said,
"we could have saved you a journey;
the women here are stone.
Cold hardens their blood,
you can see it in their eyes.
And as for the men," he stared
down the queue and all heads bowed,
"most are religious fanatics
who beg for a living.
Look at him!" he said, jabbing
the old pilgrim beside me.
"Would Buddha really want
to meet a scarecrow like this?"

The man was dusty,
and his clothes reeked
of rancid butter-oil
from praying at shrines.
But this dusty old soul
was the Buddhist lama
I had met that first day
in Darjeeling.
When he saw me,
he joined his hands
and bowed his head
in greeting.

At the next bend in the road
I waited to meet the Lama.
Not just to greet him
or to ask him the way,
but to tell him I was sorry
he was so insulted.
"Insulted?" he said. "No,
Lama Doshi was *blessed*.
The little soldier is right,
but Lord Buddha understands
and happily, again today,
in the lash of a soldier's tongue,
he has confirmed –
for he guides in mysterious ways –
I am still on the road home."

21

*Air*


Parts of this country are like County Clare :
the old stone walls, the ghosts in the wind.
I might nearly be happy living here,
but what I miss in the evening is salt in the air.

I was raised on a small northern island.
There're days I like to stand looking at waves,
grey sky falling as far as the eyes can see.
When I told all this to Lama Doshi, he said,

"Ah yes, you might nearly be happy living there,
but what you'd miss in the morning is a great
mountain, something to take the bare
look off the sky, the sadness out of the air."

## Lobsang's Story

*I think each time Lobsang*
*tells these stories he adds*
*a weed here, a stone there,*
*so they are always growing.*

Once, making my way home
over the mountains,
I was caught in a blizzard
and sheltered in a cave.

I smelt the dark for bears,
then settled in for the night,
knowing there wasn't even
a monastery near.

To pass the time I prayed
or did nothing at all :
counted the leaves on a weed,
fiddled with stones.

And all was quiet
until late in the night,
when the ghost of a herdsman
entered the cave.

I was delighted to see him,
but worried
I might have
disturbed his grave.

"Are you dead?"
I asked,
"No",
the herdsman said.

"I've just spent the morning
grazing my yak on the hills,
and I have stepped in here
out of the mid-day sun".

"And you,"
the herdsman asked,
"are you dead?"
"No," I said.

"I am on my way
to Namche Bazar,
and I am sheltering
out of a storm."

"Ah," he said, "you
are on the Tesi Pass
in winter and I am on
the high plains in summer."

*I think the last time*
*Lobsang told that story*
*it was a yak*
*that entered the cave.*

## Prayer Guide

The beads Lobsang uses to count his prayers
are made from the bones of his father's hands.

Each time he comes to the end of a prayer, he slips
a piece of smooth white bone through his fingers

then begins his chant all over again;
his father's hand still guiding the way.

## Ghosts in the Air

Just when I've got used to the chanting
we've entered the season of pipes and bells,
of drums that bang at odd hours –
it is a weird form of praying.

You would want to hear Lama Doshi
blowing on a huge Tibetan pipe :
it is the wail of the Banshee
wakening the dead from sleep.

Now I have always believed
that we live with spirits
about us, but I've never felt
so many ghosts in the air.

It is as if the dead have heard
the monks' clamorous prayers
and are returning home
through the monastery walls.

## The Vision

When the Chinese army over-ran Tiber in 1951, my mother
had a vision. She saw me married to a man who would leap
naked from the bed to chase a yak from the door. She said,
she was moving to the window, to follow the young man -
to follow the vision – when she was woken by Chinese
voices, and dragged from the bed. Later that day my father,
along with many other Tibetans, was shot for his beliefs; his
body taken from the house and burned, along with his holy
texts and prayer robes. That night my mother took me over
the high mountain passes into Nepal; to her sister's house
near Darjeeling.

The night before I became Lobsang's wife, I was sipping
sweet-tea in the kitchen when my mother told me her story;
her half-vision as she called it. She said she had asked all the
members of the family if, on that terrible night, any of them
had been given the other half of it. But, sadly, it seemed to
be lost. "It may," she said, "have been given to your grand-
mother or to one of the holy Lamas. So many had been slain.
Girl," she said, taking my face in her leathered hands, *that's
the touch I feel, when I think of her now*, "whether the vision
was a warning of good or evil, be ready for that winter
morning. For I know it was winter, because the last thing I
saw before that wart of a Chinaman dragged me from bed
was snow on the ground."

As cold a morning as any other, threads of ice in my hair. I'm woken by Lobsang leaping naked from our bed, to chase a yak from the door. He shouts, kicks its hairy hide, curses it for a demon. I hurry to the window to watch his cheeks bob up and down all along the lane. Then go to fetch the blanket from the chest. The blanket I have been sewing for this very moment, since the day I married him. Three years ago next spring. No children yet.

Lobsang has the yak out of the potato field and back on the hills. He looks so strange : naked man alone in this white wilderness. I go to him. As I wrap the blanket around him I melt the ice on his lips, take his cold into me. Here it was, the other half of my mother's vision. And I, for the first time, tell Lobsang her story. Perhaps, I say, we should return to bed and not move from the house for the rest of the day. But, this shivering man, Lobsang, laughs, dances like a bird.

He tells me that the night the Chinese entered Tibet his mother was sleeping by the fire, when, suddenly, she heard a woman wailing and a vision entered her, and – even though I was not yet born – she saw me giving you our first child. She said she saw you and me lying on a blanket. But we were not in a bedroom or a kitchen, not even in a hay-shed : we were in the middle of a snow covered field filled with yaks. And the eagles, and the mountains, and the clouds were watching us – and we were both naked and laughing.

## Her Pilgrimage

When I was a child,
other children thought
me strange. When they drew
mountains or rivers,
I drew shapes they'd never seen.
I drew whales.

No one from our village
had ever been to the sea.
So when my mother saw
the monsters I drew
she took me on pilgrimage
to Namche.

I was filled with the journey,
until a Lama – a man who knew
the world – told my mother :
"She draws whales because
the sailor reborn in her
still thinks about the sea.

I have seen children come
from high in the mountains,
who draw only pyramids.
And once, when I was a young
disciple in the monastery,
I met a child who drew only
the turtle and the lizard;

he even played a yak's horn
as if it were a didgeridoo. And though
this child was no more than four,
I felt his soul was ancient as dust;
from him I learnt to use
the short time we're given.
But a child like yours,
a child with the sea in her,
she knows the breath of a wave
is the mantra of the land,
and takes the shape life gives her."

"Ah yes," my mother sighed,
"though she holds great life,
she herself needs to be held
like water in my hands."
With that, the holy man
blessed me with sand,
juniper and incense,
to find the earth in me.

And now I'm Lobsang's wife.
Standing at the window,
watching him chop wood,
I carry his child within me.
When I am old
I will tell this child my story :

how I went to Namche;
how, even though a Lama
found the land in me,
there were times
when oars dipped through the clouds,
when I was the sea
and the moon was my mother watching
through her great whale's eye.

## Bird

*for Ita Kelly*

This morning a bird sang in the bare orchard
and I thought of you planting apples
and cranberries on your mother's silk shirt;

each red berry placed careful as a cat's paw,
yet mottled like the moon.
Frida Kahlo drew women weeping.

But you gave me the shirt off your mother's back,
painted as if it were an exotic bird;
sleeves flayed like yellow-feathered wings.

On this day I complete my fortieth year.
And each time I walk away from your paintings
what haunts is how we both clothe our ghosts.

## Hat

One evening, after he'd finished praying,
I asked Lama Doshi if he liked poetry.
"I never read it," he said, "but I love
when it greets me on the street.

This morning I spent hours arguing
with Mr Ho about the price,
and the meaning, of a new hat :
he knows I choose my own cloth.

This year I wanted none
of his Chinese greys and blues.
I wanted a hat with gold, purple,
saffron, the yellow of a butter-cup,

the red of a dragonfly :
so that even a stranger,
passing at a distance,
could see the poet in me."

## The Journey Home

*i.m. Augustine Canavan*

Some mornings
from my window
I can hear,
high up in the mountains,
the bell the monks ring
to call them to pray
for who they were,
who they are,
and who they will become,
on the journey home.

And some mornings
I join them in prayer,
imagining my own journey :
how far I've travelled
with so much baggage.
But the higher I've climbed
into the mountains,
the more I have discarded.

Let me tell you why I've come
to this ledge on a mountain,
this window on the snow-line :
it is to meet the ghost
who lives inside of me,

a man or woman I have not
seen for centuries, whose face,
whose voice, whose touch
I have forgotten,
but who knows my fear.
This soul who holds a bell for me,
that, at my last breath,
he'll ring to guide me.

## Night Song

Snow fell all last night,
now there's silver in your hair;
woman of the house.

You wear a long skirt
and a heavy yak skin coat,
bright beads; nothing else.

You teach me mantras,
the rhythm of your body;
the Om of your soul.

You wash by the fire
and when you lift your dark hair
winter is over.

I know your husband,
know the way he looks at you;
darker eyes than mine.

I come from the sea,
he is a man from the hills;
you lie between us.

✧

In the land of snow
you share all you have, as if
possession is sin.

✧

Sometimes, late at night,
you come to my lonely room;
ask if I need you.

✧

If you come tonight
I will wrap you in warm furs
and cherish the gift.

## Kulanthapitha

Past two in the morning,
I sit listening to the wind;
it comes all the way from China
whistling that sad air –
such a lonely pilgrim.

I have heard of islands
where fiddlers take tunes
out of the frail night air,
but this wind is so cold
it could not enter the soul.

Lobsang's wife says
it is a restless wind
heading for Kulanthapitha,
which she translates as
*end of the habitable world.*

## *Now that I am almost dead . . .*


Now that I am almost dead
the ghosts in corridors
hold no fear for me.
I feel I know them.
They are teaching me to whisper,
to listen to others' conversation
as if I am not there. To leave
and enter rooms unnoticed; to fade.
And I can feel a ghost growing inside me.
What is hard is the loneliness,
the learning to live without dreams.

I walk the rooms at night
while others sleep,
knowing the skin that fits me now
will never fit so well again,
that my blue eyes will fade,
that my voice will soon be quiet.
And if I could wish,
it would be that when I die
your ghost still floats inside me,
and we haunt these rooms together,
or sleep eternally under a mountain,
the clay our blanket.

## A Habitable Place

*'There is no place on earth where death cannot find us – even if
we constantly twist our heads in all directions as in a dubious and
suspect land . . .'* **Montaigne**

Reach inside of me;
through the clay, through the forest,
deep into the clouds.
Open me; there's only sky,
one restless bird flying west.

All winter I dreamt
of a habitable place
to melt skin on skin;
lovers held warm as feathers,
cradled from the curse of ice.

The sky was empty
when I found the dead blackbird;
a sort of singing
gone forever with the wind.
Pray for us who have no wings.

Another evening
waiting for the light to die;
gone, almost grey now.
If I liken you to cloud
there is no sky can hold you.

The grave still open,
all its crumbling earth still damp,
and my mother's breath,
cold as the trees in winter,
frozen on her last word 'home'.

No gift for talking.
Yet she'd hear the dead whisper :
a sea of stories;
where they lived or where they died;
chatter of distant voices.

I wake in the night,
my mother's voice at my ear,
a river of sighs.
Darkness, the oddest country,
ghosts more living than the dead.

Must have been so old.
Must have heard other voices
and thought them the wind.
When I go down on my knees
the dust rises with my voice.

When the dust settled
I was sitting by the window
watching her dead hands;
colour was gone from her face,
as if her ghost frightened her.

I have seen her ghost,
drawing itself on the road,
in search of its grave :
testing each six feet of earth,
the north wind cold in her eyes.

✧

And when the snow falls
the hills curl in on themselves
and the rivers freeze.
You open and close your door
as if birds are in the air.

If death is a stone,
the haunted live in rivers,
gaze through fish's eyes,
and though they cry in the night
they are not blessed with voices.

The cross of evening
spreading out like a dark bird :
moon eyed, star feathered;
bright creature of this dark night –
you and I afraid of flight.

You told me of death,
said I'd climb to grasp its breath;
that I'd utter prayer;
that I'd carry my own soul
before I sank into earth.

## The Apothecary

Out of curiosity
I ask the bald apothecary –
whose room smells of garlic –

what some of his potions are.
Ask, then wish I hadn't.
*"Which are you interested in?"*

I point to green oil in a bottle,
to white cloves wrapped in muslin,
to a flight of wings hanging from the ceiling.

"Those three," he says,
"are all remedies for parting
the living from the dead.

The oil comes from snake's liver,
the cloves are wild garlic,
the wings are what is left of dried bats.

I imagine you have been dreaming
with the dead and have come
to this apothecary to be healed."

Had he been expecting me?
Did he already know
what was troubling me?

Should I tell him
that I had witnessed a sky burial
and been haunted ever since?

That at night
when I close my eyes
I see the naked body of a woman

being hacked to pieces;
that I never imagined monks
capable of such a deed.

He placed incense in a bowl,
it smelt of turf burning,
of hills after rain.

"Now," he says, "I will tell you
what you need to do. First –
you must shave your head

and rub oil into your skull.
Then you must walk
for three days in the mountains

living on bats' wings and garlic.
Then your head will stink, your breath reek,
and your skin curdle

and the spirit will think you are dying;
think you too tired to carry her –
so she will leave you in peace.

After you wash in the river
she will be in the wind again,
and you will be, as you say, *Cured!*"

## The Crossing

After the yaks came the porters
with winter in their voices;
they told of passes frozen to the North.

But we were waiting for horses
before making the crossing,
for we had old men and books
and other slow, heavy things to carry.

The wind was up and it was bitterly cold,
yet all the signs were still right :
the yaks' eyes were clear,
the dogs faced into the wind.

It would be, at least, another week
before snow covered the lower passes,
and our journey no more than a day.

But the horses never came,
and the yaks' eyes closed,
and the dogs turned round,
and the road was gone.

The porters, settling in for the winter,
when they weren't sipping tea
or praying "Om! Many Padme Hum!"
had another story to tell

of how winter stole in early
and changed the life of every traveller
who left it late to make the simple crossing
from the warmth of one door to another.

"Not a story, more a prayer,"
I heard one of the old men say.

## The Damned

*"A lovely day!"*
*"Ah yes! but we'll pay for it!"*
An Irish Greeting

"I brought seven young monks
to see you last night," Lama Doshi said.
"You couldn't have, I was in
all evening, pottering about."

"I only brought them to see you," he said,
"we stood outside and looked through the window.
They were curious to know how a man
*'eternally damned'* copes in the silence.

I had told them you believe you will
burn forever after your last breath.
Some thought it eerie the way you leaned
over the fire as you read your book.

On the way home we discussed the sin
for which you might be damned.
Most thought you must have killed a man,
but Dimsang, the boy you know well,

he suggested : you are probably damned
because you are a vain, unholy poet
who lives outside the moment
and in that place, always for yourself.

Thinking on this and on Buddha's teachings,
they agreed with Dimsang and were content.
Then they sang healing songs for you,
and I recited sacred poems to comfort your soul."

## Lobsang's Wife

For over thalf the year I live with ice
on the river, yet ice on the river
is something I've never understood :

*water asleep on water*
*is not washed*
*away.*

And on days when cloud covers the valley
I light a candle in the window,
hang sage on the door.

Lobsang,
vanishing into the mist,
says I am no more than a child.

Let him talk and curse;
for what if the cloud lifted
while he was inside its body?

Who then would mend his bones?
Bless his eyes? Who then would hear
the last words of his mantra? Listen,

as I get older what I love are mornings
when the sky clears to a deep blue
and I can see as far as mountains days away.

There are times Lobsang goes there.
Nights I should miss his voice in the room,
his face by the fire. I tell you, this time

when he returns from the hills,
I'll take his hands in mine,
and though he may

rush for his prayer wheel,
stomp like a yak,
curse me for a wife,

I'll ask him
then and there,
what's this snow that covers our lives?

## Blue Bowl

*for Paula Meehan*

What she did
with all the blue bowls
I was never too sure,
but every time she went away
she brought one home.

When I visited,
I noticed she put
nothing in them,
and she did not
use them on the table.

I never asked her
about the bowls
for fear of offending
some tradition
I did not know about.

But this morning
I mentioned them
to her husband,
Lobsang,
and he said,

53

"When she started
to gather them,
I too was intrigued.
So, one day,
I asked her.

*Use them!* she said,
*isn't each one filled*
*to the brim*
*with the memories*
*of a pilgrimage?*

She pointed to a bowl
*That contains*
*the first days of spring,*
*and every step from here*
*to the monastery at Rongbuk.*

*And this, this tiny blue*
*bowl, is late autumn*
*on the road to Namche;*
*many icy days*
*and long dark nights.*

And did you find out
why they're always blue?
"Yes, but not from her.
On a pilgrimage of my own
I asked an old Lama.

She chooses a blue bowl
so it won't be out of place
with the others, or seem
somehow more important
when it's filled."

## From a Tibetan Journal

Unhappy again.
We drag ourselves
through the dregs
of autumn.
The hurricane-lamp
is lit all hours.
We can hardly remember
light on the hills.

Last night
was so cold
the glass
in the window
cracked.
We woke
with threads
of ice in our hair.

It took me
twenty minutes
to light the fire,
and twenty more
to warm the room,
and twenty more
to boil the water
to make the tea.

Now I sit
by the window
gazing out.
I do not dread
the winter,
each time
it comes around
I know
its old tune
a little better.

Nobody travels here
this time of year –
but look –
a man has appeared
on the mountain
waving a red flag.

One beautiful furl
and he is gone.

Still, tonight
I have an entry
for my journal :

*A matador of snowflakes,*
*a herald of winter,*
*stole my breath*
*but left his memory.*

*A Happy Day!*

## Late November

Outside a storm rumbles the air,
so we have pulled the shutters,
placed a wooden pole across the door
and laid yak skins over the frozen floor.

Lobsang's wife, waving smoke out of her eyes,
says, "Soon the storm will pass,
but then it might get colder,
and if that happens we'll be out of here."

I try to imagine what it's like on the hills :
wind lifting snow into clouds,
trees and birds frozen to stone;
a cold so sharp it could flay the skin.

How much colder before we make
for the monastery? "Don't worry,"
she says, "once ice seeps to the bone
that door will lead only into *Mystery*."

## The Old Tea Road

Today I asked Mr Ho, the man who makes hats, what he thought of Mao's treatment of writers during the Cultural revolution. He looked quietly at me for a moment, then returned to making hats.

His wife, a small woman with deep, empty eyes, asked : "How do you know Mr Ho was a writer before the Great Leap Forward? What right have you to question a humble poet? Can't you see that Mr Ho is at the end of the road, and that everything of value has already been taken from him : his pens, his paper, his books, his poems, even his peace. Oh yes, the Red Guard have replaced these things, they gave him a taste of their cold hatred; showed him fields of weeds, hills of stone; asked him to clean shit-houses. There were days when Mr Ho walked miles to collect wood for the fire, and when it snowed, the ice ate into his bones. Now, I have only one of his poems to show you, they made him burn the rest."

When I told her I had no idea Mr Ho was a poet, that I had always thought of him as a maker of fine, warm hats, she calmed a little. Then, as is traditional, she offered me tea, and told me her name was Xia. This is her story.

"First, this you must understand, my journey began in winter and I have been lost in winter ever since. I was a teacher in Peking and therefore, according to Mao, unclean: a leech on the people. What good were books and learning against a field of weeds?

"I was imprisoned by my students in the old school hall. I've lost all trace, all memory, of how long I was held there : months, years, or months that felt like years.

"My head was shaved, and I was often beaten and abused – hauled naked through the streets with slogans daubed on my body : *pig, foreigner*, or with a sign hanging from my neck : *capitalist, whore* . . . But fear was my greatest enemy : never knowing if that day I was to die. Never knowing if Mr Ho was already dead. If my children were dead. If my mother was dead. If my father was dead. If anyone out there remembered me.

"Eventually I was tried by one of the People's Committees, and found guilty of not caring for others. With beatings I had admitted this. You see, I was a quiet person, happy in the company of Mr Ho. To purge me of this crime I was exiled to China's western provinces, out to the cold, grey, foothills of the Himalayas.

"For crimes similar to mine, Mr Ho was exiled to a nearby village. He lived in a cold, draughty room with other men. I froze in the grey ice of the women's camp. For years we worked with peasants in the fields. And to those coming after us we were the peasnts : impossible to imagine people like us, daubed in mud, smelling of shite, reading a book of poems. Though even then, in the early days, Mr Ho would often recite his poems : late at night they sounded like prayers, or secrets from a past life.

"The harsh life – the fierce weather and the hard work – turned our skin to leather, the wind cut lines in it, until we had the faces of old men and women, or worse, the faces of the dead. It wasn't until mr Ho lost the use of his feet to frostbite that we were resettled here in Tibet. Two broken people dumped at the end of the road. But Mr Ho found that he could make hats, carefully, with the same grace with which he once made haiku; and, slowly, our life began again."

When I had finished my tea, Xia went with me to the door. Stepping out into the lane she said, "This is the old Tea Road from China; for the last twenty years all my news from home, all all my stories : the birth of my grand-children, the death of my grandmother and after her my mother, the marriages of my children, everything, has come down this dusty road. I tell you, often, when I am sad, I come out onto this road and walk, and dream I am taking the first steps towards home."

## Bread

### I

All evening I had watched
the women of the house
knead dough into snowy mounds,
white as the mountains around us;

their floured hands placed a great
calmness in the air –
like incense in a temple.

I loved the way they folded
each loaf in a prayer
before placing it near the fire, to rise.

### II

I was sleeping in the kitchen
when the ghost of an old woman
came from the shadows and stood
by a window filled with stars.

I wanted to ask her
why she was still stirring
when her breath was gone
but something in the air

told me – quieten.
I watched as she folded
an apron about her,
then set to making bread

with the same tucks and folds
I'd seen the other women make.
And as I watched
her floured hands bless the air

it began to dawn on me
that this was why
even in the middle of the night
the house smelt of bread.

## Home

The house I sleep in
is filled with Lobsang's prayers,
they empty my soul.

## Lobsang's Last Wish

Lobsang loves the smell
of things. He says,
when you are dying,
it is the last of the senses to leave.

So, on that particular day,
he will fill the room
with all the wildflowers
that grow along the riverbank.

Then, when the other senses
are gone, when the eyes
are blind, when the room
is hushed, when the pain

is so great he won't
even remember
to remember
to pray,

in that darkness,
the smell of a yellow
petal might bring
him back long enough

to give thanks for such
small blessings,
and die a grateful
rather than a bitter man.

# Ch'a

*– after Ho*

*Everything great on earth*
*begins as something small.*
*Lao Tzu*

**I**

Older than China
I am the memory of trees;
sip the earth from me.

I remember mist,
sunlight climbing the steep hills
leaf by silent leaf.

When I was a seed
I was drawn to a raindrop :
we made a strange brew.

Take me in silence;
I am all of the autumn,
cup me in your hands.

Warm in your fingers;
I am moments of quiet in
long conversations.

More than a prayer
on the road with the pilgrims,
by windows in rain.

## II

And if you see yourself here,
hand lifting the cup,
imagine these are your leaves :

no curse this winter, then spring,
three months of sadness,
you'll see its shadows haunting.

The house will feel empty, but
then there is passion,
cups left on the floor. Sunlight.

## *Stillness*

On still nights I hear
the songs my grandmother sang :
three sad songs of home.

## The Voyage

It is years since I last crossed
by boat to Ireland,
but tonight I am going home
over the waves.
The sky is filled with fading stars,
their light has travelled for a million years
and they are weary; the last trace
of the light that left us here.

I'd promised to be in Dublin by summer,
but it is the first of November :
the first day of winter.
The decks are icy underfoot
and there is snow in the air. Behind me,
a man is asking a woman if she loves him.
It is far too cold for such great questions.
It is an Irish night, under an Irish sky.

And I am beginning to remember this voyage :
the beer, the songs, the cigarettes;
the asthmatic wheeze of the engine
as it lifts us over another mountainous wave.
It is all up hill to Ireland :
against the tide, against the wind,
against the dark and the cold.
The journey, preparing us for the land.

## A Quiet House

Since I've moved to the hills
I've stopped sleeping naked,
but taken to planting flowers;
not just in the garden,
but in cooking-pots, buckets,
any old containers.
This year, when you return,
there will be laburnum, iris,
seven types of fuchsia,
to waken to each morning.
And I make this promise to you now :
I have done with travelling.
I am mending the wood
in the window, the tap at the sink.
I am letting the clocks run down.
This time, the house will whisper
when you sleep, and it will take, at least,
nine hours of moonlight to waken you.